*I sometimes wonder,
How will I know love
when I see it?*

*Will some one special man
come riding through—white horse or not?
I'd really like to know...*

Letters to Kristi

Ruth Harms Calkin
AND
Isabel Anders

LIVING BOOKS®
Tyndale House Publishers, Inc.
Wheaton, Illinois

Adapted from *Letters to a Young Bride* (Tyndale House Publishers, Inc. Copyright © 1985 by Ruth Harms Calkin)

Living Books is a registered trademark of Tyndale House Publishers, Inc.

Library of Congress Catalog Card Number 89-51649
ISBN 0-8423-2834-3
Copyright © 1989 by Ruth Harms Calkin
All rights reserved
Printed in the United States of America

95 94 93 92 91 90
8 7 6 5 4 3 2 1

Contents

How the Letters Began   9

Part One: I Wonder
Kristi's Poem   17
I Wonder   19
Walking Together   25
Marriage: Is It Equal?   33

Part Two: Dreams
He Can Match Every Dream   43
It Isn't Always Spring   51
Voices from the Past   59
The Story Inside   67
Lord, Please Whisper a Secret   73

Part Three: Real Love
Forgiveness Is a Beautiful Word   79
When the Door Says Welcome!   87
Listening Love   93
Take the Time   99

Part Four: Waiting Is Hard
It Will Be Worth It   105
Learn to Be Happy with More   113
It Takes a Lot of Little Things   121
In This Place, In This Hour   127
Once in a While   131

Love for a Lifetime?

I sometimes wonder,
How will I know love
when I see it?

Things all around me are broken:
like sidewalks, cracked
with edges that never meet ...

Will some one special man
come riding through—white horse or not?
I'd really like to know.

Someone to listen, day by day
and help to mend the broken places in me.
Is it possible, Lord?

God, you are real to me
here and now, in my only-ness
if you are anywhere at all ...

Will you be there also in the togetherness
of love, his and mine
forever and ever?

Love for a lifetime
seems so out of reach.
I want to learn how to
reach for the stars

with my feet still here on the ground.

Love, Kristi

How the Letters Began

The poem arrived in our afternoon mail, handwritten in Kristi's precise way, with her signature and a happy face next to her name!

Kristi's mom is a special friend of mine, and Kristi has been a significant part of my life through all her growing-up years ... through skinned knees, braces, hand-made Christmas cards, and happy hugs when we met at church each Sunday. Often we had our own special times of sharing—sometimes at her home and sometimes at ours.

I can hardly believe Kristi is now seventeen and on the brink of womanhood. But her insights in the poem made it clear she is thinking and feeling more and more in adult ways. And she wants to know about love ... the joy and sunshine of it, the promise and hope of loving one certain man—forever.

I'm so glad she still comes to me, her mother's friend, to share the secret places of her heart, to dare to ask the questions that you somehow find difficult to put to your mother!

It's such a confusing world today, and even in her loving Christian home with all the support Kristi has had, she's apprehensive. Especially as she prepares to leave home and family and her local Christian community for her first year in college.

The world is bombarding her with choices—so many of them extremely attractive. Sexy toothpaste smiles, bathing suits that tease at baring it all, fast guys in faster cars....

Too much, too fast can rob her of these beautiful growing years when her body has been developing in its own marvelous way along with her mind and personality. Kristi is considering the many choices and learning to select only those parts of the "good life" that she can live with honestly—rejecting those that are a cheat, that would rob her of life in its fullness.

I long to share with her what I've learned through thirty years of lasting love. I want to meet her in her doubts and dreams—and in her poetry. For she knows that I too am a poet, and we both feel at home in the language of the heart.

My husband Rollie and I have been married for thirty exciting, testing, exuberant years. That's hard to realize! I have discovered, however, that there is always more to learn about love, *much* more, especially about the ways God's love touches us at each stage of life, making it richer and better.

On the phone I extended an invitation to Kristi to have tea with me the next afternoon—just the two of us. It was obvious that she was excited and a little nervous, too.

But that's how they began, these letters to Kristi
... conversations and letters about love.

When Kristi arrived she had a blue spiral notebook
under one arm and an oversized handbag hanging
from her shoulder. She had been saving up
thoughts, questions, poems to share—and I knew
that it would be my privilege to hear the fresh,
honest seeking of a very special friend.

As we sat at the counter in my yellow kitchen
eating lemon cookies and sipping hot tea, I began
to get a glimpse of the woman she would soon be.
We had fun being together again—laughing,
sharing, just as we'd done before. Our kitchen
counter had often been the focus of our jumbled
conversations.

"Ruth," Kristi began, "I just can't imagine what
love will be like. How will I know when I meet the
right man? It seems like all the guys who want to
ask me out really don't interest me—the real
inside me, the me they can't truly know about. And
the ones I think I'd like to get to know better don't
notice *me!* Will our relationship ever be equal—
the caring, the love? I just can't imagine how!"

"Well, Kristi, sometimes first impressions make
sense—but it could be that one of those guys who
is looking your way is just as interesting *inside* as
you are. That's why dating gives us a chance to find
out, gradually, if we want to see more of a person,

or increase the commitment.... You are a beautiful person, Kristi, a thinker, and someone who feels deeply, too. I know you committed yourself to Christ when you were very young. No wonder the superficial things aren't enough for you. Money and looks and flashiness and popularity for their own sake seem empty.

"A special someone *will* appreciate the depth in you—but it may take time. For now, you're going to college! You will get to know lots of people, male and female, in many different situations. You can learn from each person up to a point. You can listen and evaluate, and you can have fun without sacrificing your integrity. You don't *have* to promise anyone anything yet. You will find how hard it is to wait, but try to think of your freedom to grow and learn as a very special privilege!"

"Can I write to you, Ruth—tell you about what I'm learning, the people I meet and decisions I'm making? It will seem less lonely. May I even share my journal with you?"

"Of course, Kristi. I'd love that! And I'll be happy to share some of my prayer journal with you so that we can compare notes. I'd like to include some thoughts from the many letters I get, too ... and my poems! Writing poems is one way I feel very close to God and his Word. It's so helpful to write my prayers and my thoughts of him, day by day."

"That helps me, too! Oh, Ruth, I have so much to learn!"

"So do I, Kristi," I said sincerely, as I reached over and gave her a big hug. Her eyes were so serious. *Lord, she is so eager to know your will,* I prayed silently. *Thank you for this friendship.*

When we got to my front door, she pulled a folded-up sheet out of her notebook and handed it to me shyly. "To Ruth, with love," it said on the outside.

I tucked the paper away and promised to savor it later.

And so the letters began. Surprisingly, they continued for many months.

Letters about living and learning and loving . . . letters about laughter and tears . . . about trusting and praying . . . about sharing and listening and forgiving . . . about growing and knowing.

Letters about the rich and beautiful things God longs to give us when he is invited to live in our lives, to be a part of our dreams and hopes—including the hope of someday sharing our love with one special person.

ONE *I Wonder*

Kristi's Poem

A friend is someone who is there
across the table, just next door . . .
a voice on the phone, a note in the mail.
I can't see love—
does it have a face?
But yours speaks to me, here and now.
A heart to listen,
words to answer,
are meat and drink on the way.
Thank you for *you*
as we share the steps ahead.

I Wonder

Dear Kristi,

You should see the notes cluttering my desk! Corners of envelopes, a few note cards, a paper napkin, even a small brown sack—all with hurriedly scribbled reminders of things I want to share with you.

The truth is thoughts of you are no small thing around here. You've pushed and pulled at my heart ever since our last visit together. I do laundry, make the bed, dust furniture, and suddenly I picture you doing some of the same things in your new dorm room. You probably have your mind on a lot more exciting things in your life at college, but eventually you *will* have to dust!

Kristi, even now I can scarcely believe it. To think that we sat in my kitchen, you and I, talking about the special things God has in store for your life. What in the world happened to the years . . . the days . . . the moments? Just yesterday, it seems, we were talking about your new puppy and roller skates and Christmas programs and piano lessons.

Kristi, I'll be writing frequently as I promised. Today I'm going to share some letters from six collegians—all friends of ours. The letters express some questions and ideas relating to love.

Dear Ruth,

I've thought a lot about our conversation on love. Sometimes I get too anxious to find the "love" of my life. I just want to know *who* it's going to be ... the man who will make me stop in my tracks and say, "This is it. Don't look any farther!" Will I see it in his face—will there be some clue? What if he doesn't feel the same way about me? Will I end up with "second best"? Please help me.

Love, Karen

Dear Ruth,

I'm having too good a time dating to want to settle down, even though two of my best friends are engaged already and planning weddings. I just want to keep growing and learning for a while. I want to travel, start working as a teacher, and see what influence I can have on the lives of my students, especially as a Christian. It's almost June, and everywhere I look are pictures of brides, honeymoon vacations—even my parents seem to want me married off to a Christian man and "taken care of." I think it's different for women today and I can take care of myself! But I do want marriage and family someday. What if I get so independent I can never learn to live with someone else? I don't want to be selfish. Please answer my letter soon.

Paula

Dear Ruth,

I almost got married last year, but I broke my engagement to Mark six months before the wedding. It was a terrible scene. I know I hurt him, and I felt awful. But it just wasn't right. He is really a fine person, but I felt like I was suffocating in the relationship. He couldn't understand. I can see I have a lot to learn before I'm ready to be a wife. I don't want to hurt anyone else that badly again—nor do I want to be hurt. Marriage really is serious business. It's heavier than college! I need a friend.

Love, Sheri

Dear Ruth,

I really want the woman I marry to love Christ more than she loves me. I guess I want to be able to count on her to stand firm even in my weaknesses.

I hope we will both always feel each other's prayerful support. I pray there will be a co-sharing of God's endowments to us—the fulfillment of the uncompleted "half" in both of us.

I really want her to be "easy to look at"! But I want her beauty to come from her inner life.

Above all, I want both of us to trust Christ completely.

Dru

Dear Ruth,
Everyone thinks it's so easy being the man because we can do the asking out for dates! But it's not that simple. We don't always want to take the risk of being rejected. If we don't feel someone is interested already, it's scary to just offer our company and get turned down flat. I wish I could meet a Christian young woman who is interested in the things that interest me and serious about seeking God's will for her life. Somewhere I hope I'll find the right wife for me.

Rick

Dear Ruth,
I'm thankful that God is first in Jon's life. That's what first made me notice him. His honesty and leadership qualities attracted me, too. He enjoys simple things like flying a kite or an afternoon drive. Especially now that he is my fiancé, he shows me I'm special in a thousand ways. This *is* love. Can it last forever? I hope so!

Gail

Kristi, what these collegians seem to be asking is: What is love like, and how will I know it? How does being a Christian make a difference?

Years ago, while sitting under a sprawling oak tree on my university campus, I wrote a letter to Rollie, telling him again of my love for him, as we approached our wedding day. I haven't always lived up to my high goals as a wife. I've failed a thousand times. God knows this, and so does Rollie. But I am loved, and I'm so thankful to share my life with him.

Right now you are living on a beautiful tree-lined campus. On a sunny day, why don't you grab a pencil, find your own sprawling tree, and write a letter. Write about the kind of wife you want to be someday, and about the qualities you hope to find in a husband. I can't wait to hear your thoughts and hopes as you settle into a brand new life at college!

P.S. Thank you for your beautiful poem! I'm eager to see more. . . .

Walking Together

Dear Ruth,

Thank you for sharing some of your letters with me. It's good to know I'm not alone in my questions and wondering. Because of you, I feel like I have a friend even when I walk alone around this campus.

This morning I read from Psalm 32:8: "I will instruct you and teach you the way you should go; I will counsel you with my eye upon you" (RSV).

Ruth, I really need to know that the man I marry will also know God in this way, so we can walk together.

Yesterday, I wrote this poem:

Two Together

There are two sides to a coin,
two eyes to a face,
two hands and two feet;
a "one" and an "other."

God made man and then woman
to work on the earth,
to build and to plant
and to love one another.

> When two walk together
> they must agree.
> It's God who can help them
> be one with each other.

Ruth, it's so hard to hold onto a Christian view of marriage today when all around you homes are breaking up. Divorce happened to Steve's parents—he's the guy I dated for a while last year. It's very confusing. His dad was on the church board, but he left his family! I don't understand how a Christian can do that—hurt so many people close to him. Why does God let these things happen?

Love, Kristi

Dear Kristi,
I'm sitting at the round maple table in our dining room. Two crazy little birds are singing their hearts out on our front lawn, each trying absurdly to out-sing the other. Their chirping adds a melodic descant to my clicking typewriter.

The password this morning is *joy!* Joy laughing and singing and chasing sunbeams all over the hills. There's something nostalgic in the atmosphere, something exciting. I don't know what, exactly. The subtle fragrances, perhaps—or the warm September sun. Maybe it's the blazing panorama of color: orange, scarlet, gold, wherever you look.

Or maybe it's just that today happens to be

the third of September—our wedding anniversary!

Can you believe that, Kristi? Thirty years. What a lot of living two people can do in that amount of time! What a lot of sharing and caring and laughing and crying. What a lot of love—*what an immense amount of love.*

The other day a friend asked, "Knowing what you know now about marriage, the good and the bad, the ups and downs, would you do it all over again?"

I couldn't help but smile. My eager response was, "If I could marry the same husband—yes. I'd start tomorrow. No, I'd start today!"

This morning at the front door, after a strong male kiss, Rollie grabbed me and said, "I love being committed to you!" I probably looked startled. I don't remember that he's ever said it quite like that before. Usually he says, "I love being married to you," but this was different. I've been thinking about the words all day: *I love being committed to you. . . .*

A commitment, Kristi, is a vow, a pledge, a *promise*—and our attitude toward commitment has a very important bearing on our attitude toward marriage.

When I was little, it was my mother who first taught me the intrinsic value of a promise. She was an exceptional teacher. Her lessons were always taught in the most impressive way—by personal example.

We learned very early in our family about Mother's integrity. Whenever we wanted to go somewhere or do something special, we knew exactly when our wish would be granted: the moment we could persuade her to say "I promise."

Words like *maybe* or *perhaps* or *we'll see* were wobbly words. The decision could go either way. But a promise was as sure as sunshine, as certain as six o'clock. It never occurred to us to remind Mother of a promise or to ask again. We knew—we always *knew*—we'd go to the circus, or we'd stay overnight with a friend, or we'd pop popcorn after dinner, or whatever. Once having committed herself, that was it. A promise was a promise, made solemnly in good faith, and carried out despite weariness, inconvenience, or personal sacrifice.

Mother was eager to instill her conviction in us! Her emphatic words still brush against my memory: "Never say 'I promise' unless you really intend to keep your word." Then, with a twinkle in her blue-gray eyes, she would add, "Remember, a promise is for keeping!" Her oft-repeated words left a permanent imprint on my life. I began to learn at an early age something of the meaning of commitment.

Hundreds of times in our marriage Rollie and I have made promises. The word *commitment* is as much a part of us as the furniture in our home. No, much more. The furniture could be demolished tomorrow.

But thirty years ago, before God and to each other, we made a life commitment. "As long as forever is"—that was our vow—our settled decision. We didn't slide into it, nor did we crawl or drift into it. There was nothing casual or careless about it. With our minds, our wills, and our hearts wide open, we pledged. Willingly and openly we assumed a personal responsibility. We were accountable to each other.

Our commitment involves our investment of time and talent and energy. It means vulnerability. It involves our moods, our risks, our personal choices—our dreams and disappointments.

Commitment involves our love, rich and abiding, bigger by far than we had ever dreamed. Where there is genuine love, there is freedom. Freedom to express, to respond, to listen, to learn. Love eliminates a grin-and-bear-it acceptance. Commitment is love doing, love giving, love acting without a thought of quitting.

It is a serious thing to make a commitment to someone else. It puts enormous demands on us. Commitment tests our patience, our integrity, our vitality, and tests our ability to adjust—to accept each other without reservation. Marriage deals with real problems, with real decisions, with real conflicts—but so does all of life!

Granted, we take a few tumbles along the way. We stub our toes and skin our knees from time to time. But nobody with an ounce of courage ever stops in the middle of a venture because of a skinned knee.

Kristi, I feel very sad about Steve's family. I pray for his mother and sisters and for Steve every day. And I pray for his dad, because he must be in a lot of pain, too. Why do some people give up and quit? I don't know. But God does allow us to fail—he has given us free will to choose his way and walk with him, or fall aside from his will. What we all need to remember is that God's way is *true freedom.*

My friend Mark said one day, "Doesn't a commitment bind you? Don't you feel chained by it?" On the contrary, a commitment frees us to explore, to climb, to keep our eyes on the goal. Enticing detours simply lead to dead ends. We may do some heavy trudging, but that's when we depend upon God and upon each other the most.

Kristi, I believe our love continues to grow because our commitment to each other *is* superseded by another commitment: our personal commitment to God. Your lovely poem expresses this truth. Years ago Rollie and I discovered that we simply could not be God to each other. It is utterly impossible for any couple to find in each other what can be found in God alone. How insecure we would be if our dependency centered on anyone or anything that we could lose.

But God is our security—God who can never be lost! In marriage the greater commitment to God makes the lesser commitment to each other as shining as silver and as durable as gold.

The thing that makes it so wonderful is this: The One to whom we are committed is eternally committed to us. We have his assured word for it: "In everything you do, put God first, and he will direct you and crown your efforts with success" (Proverbs 3:6, TLB).

From My Journal

Commitment means
we take the very worst of each other,
the very best of each other,
and the in-between of each other;
then, stirring it all together,
we say with gentle understanding,
"I love and totally accept
the mixture of you."

Marriage: Is It Equal?

Dear Ruth,

I read these words today in Ephesians 5:22: "Wives, submit yourselves unto your own husbands, as unto the Lord" (KJV). And I wrote in my journal:

It sounds like handing someone else a blank check with my name signed at the bottom! Could I ever trust anyone enough to do that? Lord, if this is your way, I want to understand it and live up to it when I commit myself to the man that I marry. But what if I'm right about a decision and my husband is wrong?

How can I agree to submit ahead of time without knowing what it will require of me in the future?

Lord, I believe your Word stands forever and is always true for our lives. But now women are doing so much more—making decisions, working at jobs and professions every day, earning money. Does that change the whole idea of *submission* somehow?

I really want to know how to be a woman today—and eventually a wife. Will my husband listen to me when I have good ideas? I want to use my mind and write books someday! Will some man be secure enough to accept that part of me and love me for my gifts and desires too? I will want *him* to succeed in his work. Why should it seem any different for him to accept my gifts—especially my success if it comes?

Dear Ruth, can you make any sense of this? I'm confused, and I'm not even planning to be a wife anytime soon. Please tell me, do you consider yourself a *submissive* wife?

Love, Kristi

Dear Kristi,
Your letter is here on my desk—the letter in which you asked directly, "Do you consider yourself a *submissive* wife?" You may not remember, but you underscored the word *submissive* with a bold stroke of your pen.

Did it occur to you that you might be asking the wrong person? I have a feeling Rollie would be your most reliable source. Believe me, he could come up with some fascinating details after thirty years of living with me.

But I want to tell you my honest conviction about the biblical principle you refer to in Ephesians 5. I am personally persuaded, on the basis of the Bible, that submission is an *attitude*—the recognition of masculine leadership in marriage. It is my willingness to accept the authority God has entrusted to my husband. It is indeed a trust.

Through the years I have learned, and I'm still learning, that when I submit to my husband's leadership in areas for which God holds him directly responsible, the path is amazingly smooth. Our relationship is restful and satisfying, and my sense of fulfillment peaks. I am not incessantly trying to prove something to myself or anyone else. I can live with myself contentedly. I have a sound basis for praying, "God, I don't ask you to take sides. Just take over."

The verse in Ephesians in no way suggests that women are inferior. It simply gives us a clue that men and women *do* function somewhat differently in marriage. Yes, we are equal before God, and our worth, our work, our desires are equally important. But the family is a very special domain, and within it, I believe the Bible teaches that men are called to be leaders and protectors in many ways, even in today's society. Perhaps men today don't go out to stalk wild beasts for dinner or physically fend off enemies! But a man's strength is different in some ways from a woman's; his body is different. He has a different emotional makeup. And although today more men and women are switching roles, as breadwinner or stay-at-home parent, for instance, these switches only *underline* the norm: that usually women are called to a primary role of nurturing, and men to the role of support and sustenance.

Then there are families in which the men have left, such as Steve's. In many cases women are having to carry both roles, and it's very difficult.

Not at all as God intended. By God's grace, in such a circumstance of loss, either parent can find the strength to carry on, with hard work and integrity.

But here in Ephesians 5 we are looking at the ideal. And what an ideal it is!

I believe that when the time comes, you will be able to see, in your own particular circumstances, *how* you are being called to submit to your husband: whether to adapt your life to his work situation and earning power, to his spiritual leadership, or to his ability to make wise decisions in times of stress. Yes, it does sound like a blank check, and that *is* scary! Frankly, I am very strong-minded about what I want out of life, and over the years I haven't always been sure about the idea of being a submissive wife either!

However, seldom has decision making caused a major conflict in our marriage. Usually we are able to come to an agreement without a catastrophe. I remember a time when we were totally divided on an issue. I had sufficient wisdom to *say* little and *pray* much. However, my talk with God was certainly slanted toward *my* opinion: "Lord, I think Rollie is completely mistaken. Please talk to him. Whatever it takes, help him to change his mind. You know how determined he is, so you'd better work fast!"

I was writing my paper that morning (as I so often do), and right at the end of the sentence there came the convicting thought, *Don't ask me to make your husband what you want him to be. Just ask me to make him what I want him to be.*

What do you do with an admonition like that? Well, if you're wise, you *obey* it.

As it happened, Rollie was right. But he isn't always. Decision making involves risk. No husband is infallible. No wife is infallible. There may be errors in judgment, an occasional wrong choice. At times a wrong choice may bring drastic complications. At such times we have to encourage and support each other. A bitter "I told you so" in no way corrects the damage. It only builds a wall of isolation.

We've found that God is able to make even a wrong choice contribute to our highest good when our motivation is sincere and when our loyalty to each other is intact.

Does the principle of submission devalue my potential? Not at all. Do I make decisions? Certainly. Without always running to my husband? Of course. Does he trust me? In some areas more than he trusts himself!

I am certainly not thwarted or confined. I am not pushed aside like an ornament after Christmas. My capabilities are not shelved. Rollie supports my work as a writer completely. He is my biggest "fan"! I am a woman—with a legitimate right to my individuality. How is all this possible? Well, Paul goes on to say: "For the husband is the head of the wife, even as Christ is the head of the church. . . .

Husbands, love your wives, even as Christ also loved the church, and gave himself for it."

I have a profound appreciation for the two little words *even as*. They indicate that a husband is to exert his leadership with the genuine love and compassion of Jesus Christ. What enormous implications! Think about it, Kristi—*could any wife ask for more?*

I'll never forget Rollie's prayer one morning at the breakfast table: "Lord, make me the husband you want me to be—first for your sake, then for Ruth's sake."

We were having waffles for breakfast, and as I poured the syrup, I felt my heart pouring out as well. I could trust a husband who prayed like that.

Ephesians 5:21 is literally loaded with gold nuggets. Here's still another: "Honor Christ by submitting to each other" (TLB). In other words, Paul is letting us know that submission is not a muddy one-way street for wives only. The husband is not the undisputed czar in his home who makes arbitrary decisions without an ounce of concern for his wife. A wife need not stifle her intellect or repress her ideas for fear of deflating her husband's masculinity.

I know what you're thinking. I can feel the vibrations all the way from your campus to my kitchen. Thoughts like: *Wonderful! Beautiful! I'm all for it! But where in all the world is there a husband who reflects the unconditional love of*

Christ all the time? Where is there a wife who joyfully submits, never tangling or wrangling with her own emotional conflicts? I mean—after all!

Yes, Kristi, I know, no one ever lives up to this ideal. None of us succeeds every hour of every day. We're vulnerable, susceptible, moody, and too often contentious.

Nevertheless, there is the goal. Or rather, Christ is the goal! His love in our lives, in our marriage makes the difference. When we put no limits on him, he shows us the way. Then he enables us to *act* on what he reveals. The wonderful truth is that the more we both submit to Christ, the more joyfully we will submit to each other!

It *is* the only way two can walk together, Kristi, as you have put it. I believed this truth from the time Rollie and I were married, but with a few ominous clouds hovering over my rebellious spirit. Today I believe it with unwavering conviction. It works—as God has said in his Word that it does.

In my next letter I want to tell you how I learned in a drastic, painful way to submit to my husband's spiritual leadership. It happened a long time ago, but the memory of it is still vivid. Don't be alarmed—it all turned out beautifully!

Love, Ruth

TWO Dreams

He Can Match Every Dream

Dear Kristi,

I'm having a struggle with myself today as I write this letter to you. I promised to share my personal battle of long ago, but as I begin to put it down, black print on white paper, I'm suddenly aware that you will have a grim and glaring revelation of me. But here goes....

Before we were married, Rollie's major at the University of Oregon was in commercial art, and I loved everything about it. I had lavish dreams for our future.

Often we'd go to the campus together, and I'd sit for hours on a tall wooden stool, pensively watching as flaming colors splashed over his canvas. Frequently I'd envision the home we'd have—a home of elegant style and charm. I was sure commercial artists earned enormous salaries, and my husband was bound to succeed.

It wasn't that I'd minded my childhood's old-fashioned parsonages with their high ceilings, heavy sliding doors, and walk-in pantries. Even as I write to you, I remember friendly kitchens and cobwebby attics and damp basements (cellars, we called them).

But life was different now. I wanted to be sophisticated and even wealthy. I longed to see the world from the other side. Of course, to see it with Rollie was my fondest dream.

Our wedding was beautiful, and after a glorious five-day honeymoon we returned to give our small, unsuspecting apartment a radical face-lift. We attempted things we'd never tried before. Our spirits overflowed with adventure, and every innovation seemed to call for another.

One day as we were covering the couch with new fabric, I said blissfully, "Oh, Honey, before too long we'll be able to buy a *new* couch. Won't it be wonderful?" He smiled.

Then unexpectedly everything came crashing down on my dreams. A new development left me groping and grasping. I simply wasn't prepared for what happened next.

It was about lunchtime, and Rollie came dashing through the front door of our small apartment, glowing with excitement.

As I write to you now, Kristi, I can still remember the vibrancy in Rollie's voice as he shouted the "good news." He had been invited to join the staff of the First Baptist Church of Eugene (our home church at that time) as minister of music and Christian education. Wasn't it miraculous?

Frankly, no! In no way did this fit into my satin-lined box of personal dreams. I bluntly said so.

I knew that Rollie had often prayed for such an opportunity, long before we were married. I knew too of the quiet morning he had utterly committed his life to God. Anything . . . anywhere . . . always . . . he had vowed. There had been no shaking, bulldozer changes in his life—just the confident trust that God had heard. Rollie had continued his major, but always with the hopeful thought of something more. Was God now giving us a fleeting glimpse of the future? Undoubtedly my husband thought so.

I just stood there, stoical and unresponding.

I finally managed to come up with something dramatic and curt (I'd probably read it in some magazine): "So this is the way a girl's dream comes to an end—all in a moment, just like that." I snapped my fingers.

Rollie's response was less dramatic but far more effective. "Honey, we can't disregard God's direction. We both know that. He'll show us the way if we let him, and I'm willing for the change to be in me. But we *must* be together. Will you talk to him with me?"

The following morning I found a note on the breakfast table.

> Darling . . . your happiness is more important to me than anything in the world. I'm willing to invest energy, time, money, everything in our

marriage. I have pledged myself to take care of you always.

Sometimes, I suppose, I'll have to make decisions on my own, and I'll count on you to stand by me. Undoubtedly you will make some decisions on your own, and I'll stand by you. But *this* decision is one we absolutely must make together.

I've often told you of the strange urgency within me. I think it started the day I sat in your father's office and we talked for several hours. This was even before you and I were dating. Since then, I've never been free from wondering if God had something more for me—and now for us. That's why we must consider the invitation that has come.

However, this is to let you know *I will not force the issue.* It would never work. God will show us both. I will not give any answer until we come to a mutual agreement—however we decide. In the meantime, please know I love you with all of my being.

That day, although I wasn't conscious of it, God was launching an intensive training program in our lives. He was teaching us the particular steps of submission he required of us both at that time. If we were to gain new ground together, we simply could not be spiritually divided.

The next few weeks were miserable and lonely. I felt hedged in, pushed about, as I kept bumping into concrete walls of my own selfishness.

Rollie was kind and gentle—and very, very careful with me. When we talked, he didn't press the issue or point out my weakness or lack of faith. We both knew we couldn't go into the ministry with a halfway commitment. Rollie patiently waited for God's timing.

During the stretched-out weeks I kept tripping over the words my father had frequently quoted: "One who does the will of God abides forever."

Relentlessly God kept hitting me where it hurt. Every song, every sermon, every word became a painful stab. I could hide the Bible under the bed or in a drawer, but I couldn't quiet the echo in my struggling heart.

Then one damp October day I finally faced God honestly and directly. I couldn't put him off any longer. To hinder his plan by my foolish rebellion was too great a risk. I began to let go of *my* idea of our future. Seriously and honestly I considered what God might want.

Before our wedding, we had invited Jesus Christ to live in our home forever. He had every right to be first, and I knew it. *Surely he could match every dream of mine!*

At last the crisis ended. Rollie had undoubtedly done a lot of private praying. Now I could tell him I wanted God's will for both of us. I could believe, or at least *begin* to believe, that God was for us, not against us.

As we talked that day, intimately and tenderly, our happiness knew no bounds. We laughed, sang, teased, loved, prayed, and praised. Then we went out and bought the biggest hamburgers we could find anywhere in town!

Have we been disappointed? Has life cheated us? Have we missed out on the good life? No, no! Not once have we regretted the decision to go into ministry. *Not once.*

God turned us around. He started us on a new path of continual service, and we have walked it *together.*

Kristi, I share this with you because you are at a stage of your life when you are making important decisions that can change your life course forever! Even before you meet the person you want to share your life with, it's not too soon to give your heart completely over to God's way. As your own commitment increases, and your life becomes deeper and richer, this will help determine *who you are*—and the kind of man who will be attracted to you—who will, in fact, want to link his life with yours. Your standards, when it comes to submission to God's will, can never be too high!

I pray for you every day.

Love, Ruth

Dear Ruth,
Thank you for sharing that story with me! It's hard to believe you were ever rebellious! This helps me to know that God works with us as we are. I have so many dreams and hopes, too. And I want to share them someday with a man who also loves the Lord. Do you think he's really out there—maybe even walking around on this campus? I wonder....

Love, Kristi

It Isn't Always Spring

Dear Ruth,

Is God There?

An empty mailbox—no letter from home...
Two dollars left to make it to Friday...
Faces everywhere, people going their own
   way...
A smile or two, maybe, but not a Friend.
Emptiness is like a black hole, some days.
I walk carefully, so I won't fall in.

But up above, the sky is still in place;
stars are there to reach for.
God is there, and also here, beside me.
I wish I could see, I wish I could feel
just a *little* more ... please, Lord,
say my name.

Dear Ruth,
Sometimes I feel like I need so much more than
I'm getting—more love (even though my family—
and you—let me know you really care). I long to
be close to someone in the way you talk about in
your letters. I've met a few people I enjoy going to

the library with, sometimes lunch, things like that. I've even had a couple of dates, to a concert and our class picnic. These things are fun and encouraging. But, I have to admit, marriage sounds terribly appealing—to be able to *count on* one special person—a permanent date! I've seen enough of the marriages in our town, even our church, to know it isn't a perfect answer to anything. But it sure sounds better than the loneliness I'm feeling now.

Love, Kristi

Dear Kristi,
Remember this old story?

"And as they rode off into the sunset, the prince promised her his love, his riches, and his castle in the clouds if only she would be his. They were married and lived happily ever after...." It sounds wonderful, I know, but don't forget, *that* version of love and marriage is a fairy tale!

All people, even couples in love, have to live out their story in the real world—the world of imperfection. The world of other people!

God gives sufficient light and strength for one day at a time, and each day has to be really *lived.* In marriage there is often the temptation to think that the *real* joy and fulfillment are just around the corner. False expectations always bring frustration. True, love helps us bear the grayness and the lean times, but in marriage it isn't always spring!

This is the unmasked reality that every couple eventually faces. Some couples make the adjustment less painfully than others, but no couple avoids it completely.

Rollie and I still have the postcard I sent to my parents thirty years ago. They saved it for us because of its rare combination of humor and naivete: "Bliss! Nothing but bliss! Day after day of uninterrupted bliss!"

I wrote that up-to-the-minute report after we had given our marriage the long enduring test of — *eleven days*.

But one sullen day about *eleven weeks* later, while rain was pouring like sheets of liquid glass, I pulled a crusted rack out of a crusted oven, stumbled over the dustpan in the middle of the floor, banged my head on an open cupboard door, and said to the walls, "So this is bliss?"

Was our marriage a tragic mistake? Was the excitement and joy of our engagement an illusive dream? Did crusted oven racks and dirty clothes and pressured schedules prove we didn't love each other? Were we "incompatible"?

No, Kristi, it simply proved we had a lot to learn. We were beginning to discover what love and marriage were all about. We had committed ourselves to something far more inclusive than either of us had dared to dream. Someday you will make the same discovery.

Author Sam Shoemaker points out that everybody

has a problem, *is* a problem, or *lives* with a problem. We can't argue with that!

So one thing is certain: Whatever marriage was meant to be, it wasn't meant to be *the answer* to our lives. Only God can be that.

Any theory about marriage which ignores stark reality isn't worth considering. Even couples in love eventually have to stoop to clean the toilet, the greasy stove, the refrigerator with the strange sour odor from two squashed tomatoes in the vegetable bin.

Take a glance at the unpolished silverware, the undusted furniture, the drooping plants that need water. Then there's the sticky syrup on the carpeting, the spoon caught in the disposal, the delicate china cup shattered to bits, the termite pellets on the closet shelf.

Do you see, Kristi? Even in marriage it isn't always spring!

But that's only part of the picture. You and your husband both may have jobs, so on foggy mornings you'll battle traffic and cautiously switch lanes and hope you can show up at the office before your boss arrives. While you creep with the traffic you'll think about mounting bills and the laundry you forgot to transfer to the dryer and the meat you should have taken from the freezer.

In marriage there are sudden emergencies, too: a crushed fender that was undoubtedly your fault. A plugged disposal on the Saturday night you're entertaining two other couples for dinner. A telephone call in the middle of the night—your mother is suddenly ill and your dad doesn't know what to do.

There are overprotective relatives and neighbors with silly complaints. Tempers flare and words slash and tears spill all over the place. Hostilities crouch in corners. You soon learn that it isn't so much what you say to each other but the tone you use when you say it.

Once in awhile fond memories will come to mind. You'll think back to the simple, carefree days when you came and went at will, when the money you earned was yours to do with as you pleased (enjoy it now!), when you didn't worry if a button was missing. Unmatched socks didn't trouble you either—that was someone else's problem.

When you wanted to get away from your family, you put the Do Not Disturb sign on your bedroom door, or you dashed into the kitchen, grabbed a cookie, and said, "Gotta run, Mom."

But when you're married, Kristi, it's different. You're accountable to each other. You're responsible. You're making a life investment in a permanent relationship. *Your* way becomes *our* way. *Earned* money is *joint* money. *My* time is *shared* time. On the run means off to work and back home to more work.

In marriage it isn't always spring!

Should that fact scare you away from marriage?

It needn't! Whether single or married, every season of life is beautiful—a gift from God. *And the secret of the seasons is balance.* We all need the tranquility of winter, the warmth of summer, the brilliance of autumn, the exuberance of spring.

Without the dishes and dusting of everyday life we'd miss the discipline. Without conflicts we'd miss happy compromises. Without problems we'd miss prayer. Without hurting we'd miss holding. Without listening we'd miss learning. Without grief we'd miss growth. Without the darkness we'd miss the dawn.

Married love is not endless bliss. It is not continued ecstasy. It is not Hawaii in May and Palm Springs in December. *Married love is genuinely wanting the highest and best for your mate*—as much as you want it for yourself. Love has no limits to its endurance. As God's Word tells us, this is the one thing that will stand when all else has fallen.

Too often "throw-away" marriages seem to be the accepted thing. But, Kristi, if you want to sustain a lifelong relationship someday (and I know you do), genuine commitment is the answer. This is not enslavement. Rather it is security even in the midst of problems and responsibilities. Love means being open and teachable even when it's not convenient. Seldom is it convenient! We learn this by *living*—slowly, steadily, sometimes painfully. And often it's the pain that deepens the love. That's what commitment is all about.

God has a lot of stars in his sky, Kristi, and they keep on shining! I believe he will show you your own shining future of love and sharing—through all the seasons of life. Remember, he'll show you *one day at a time.*

From My Journal

Marriage is a combination of salt and
    stardust—
salt for hamburgers and stardust for poetry.
You can undoubtedly survive a little longer
on hamburgers than you can on poetry;
but why settle for one
when God wants you to have both?

Voices from the Past

Dear Ruth,

Thanks so much for reminding me that marriage doesn't solve all our problems. Doesn't it seem that the more people work on their own lives and their own relationship to the Lord, the fewer problems they will bring into their marriage? I guess that's one good reason for waiting and really growing up more before you make that Big Decision.

I keep discovering more about my own personality traits, my preferences and dislikes, and the way I enjoy going about learning. (I have learned that people have different ways of listening, of gathering information, and of acting. It's fascinating!) I know that choosing a mate is more than *figuring things out*—rationally deciding what kind of man would make the best partner for me. There's also love, attraction—and most of all, God's leading. It's a mix of all of that, isn't it? Rational choice, using our head and the insight God gives, but not forgetting our heart, our feelings, our spirit. With all those parts, I'm sure it just has to be pulled together by God to really work!

I enjoy hearing about your experiences and your

wisdom after thirty years of a happy marriage.

Please write more!

Love, Kristi

Dear Kristi,

I'm proud of you, and your clear, sensible thinking about marriage. I think you've stumbled onto one important fact that is often ignored. In discovering more about yourself and accepting the beauty of the way God made *you,* a unique personality, you are also learning how the uniqueness of another person might mesh with your life. Remember, Kristi, *basically you will both be exactly the same persons after marriage as you were before marriage.* Marriage will not dissolve your personal identity. God does not intend for you and your future mate to fit into each other's mold. Your way of dealing with life, of observing and discerning and making choices is part of the way God made you. You will grow and change and meet each other in loving compromise, but you each have a separate history up to the point of your marriage. And along with your life experiences you will both bring "voices" from the past.

A young friend of mine said, "I had no idea that after our wedding we'd hear so many other voices! All of our conditioning, our moods, our clinging habits just moved right in with us—rent-free!"

Kristi, in every marriage there are inescapable echoes from the past. At times they whisper; often they shout. But if couples hear the voices with openness and gentle love, they need not damage the marriage relationship. Rather, they can push each mate on toward maturity. This is God's intention! Let me share some of the voices:

The voice of established patterns. I have a friend whose family celebrates big—they always have. Parties, picnics, the works. On her first birthday after marriage her husband gave her a tube of pink lipstick and a card—that was it. Otherwise, the day was very ordinary.

She chided herself for her disappointment. When she told me about this experience, she said, "It wasn't that I wanted an expensive gift—I just missed a real celebration."

Later her husband said with glowing pride, "Honey, I hope the lipstick was all right. That's the first time in my life I ever gave anyone a birthday gift. In my family we didn't even give cards."

The voice of hidden traits. Living together day in, day out is a revealing experience. We see each other without façade or pretense. The true self emerges. We begin to recognize traits we hadn't detected before—an assertiveness, perhaps, or stifling fear. We see temper, impatience, hostility. We see blunder and bluff. Lack of discipline becomes obvious. Often we see deep conflicts between will and emotion, between duty and desire. "For better or for worse" can be words of real challenge.

The voice of moods, habits, and manners.
Emotions are incredibly puzzling. Moods sweep us rapidly from the basement of despair to the tenth floor of exhilaration.

A meticulous bride said, "An open closet door just makes me furious!" Sometimes it doesn't take much. Habits and manners can be as irritating as tiny gnats. Lost keys, newspaper clutter, towels heaped in a corner, nervous gestures, too much food in one busy mouth, elbows slumped over the table . . .

Voices from the past!

Kristi, marriage is not a game for children. The pressures after marriage are bigger and the stakes are far higher.

At first couples are tempted to treat the voices as invited guests. They hedge. They ignore them. But the voices won't budge!

Next, some couples try force. They resort to tears or coaxing. Again it won't work. You see, the voices *like* living in a cozy home. They've known both mates for a long time.

Is there a solution, then? How can anyone learn to "live happily ever after" with such brazen interference? Let me suggest several ways:

Introduce each voice to Jesus Christ, the Lord of your home. He alone can handle the conflicts. His love transforms. His power re-creates. He will begin to mold and sharpen and refashion. He will teach you to make friends with the voices. Gradually you will discover a refreshing fact: Your strengths are probably supporting each other's weaknesses!

Refuse to let the voices drown out the verbal expression of love. "Honey, I just want to thank you for having more patience with me. I've really noticed it."

"You look wonderful today!"

"Wow! We haven't argued about money for a month. We must be growing, 'cause we don't have any more money than we had last month!"

Demonstrate love when you don't feel loving. One day I had a telephone call. A charming voice on the other end of the line said, "We're delighted that you're going to speak to our potluck tomorrow night. Do you need directions?"

I was dumbfounded. Nobody had called *me* about speaking at a potluck dinner! As it happened, Rollie had taken the message. He had graciously accepted the invitation for me on a tentative basis. I was to call back if I couldn't speak, but *Rollie had neglected to tell me*.

At that precise moment I didn't exactly feel like writing a love letter. But had anyone asked, "Do you love your husband?" my immediate response would have been, "I certainly do! If I didn't you'd never catch me in a predicament like this!"

Accept each other. Often we have faced ourselves with definite questions:

Are towels heaped in the corner really important enough to make an issue over?

Is too much food in one busy mouth just my own pet peeve, or do I desire change for the good of my mate and his other relationships?

How could I have handled this conflict more tactfully and maturely?

Is this a trait I should accept unconditionally, or may I anticipate God's creative change?

If my mate's reaction were the same as mine at this instant, would I feel hurt or resentful?

Let laughter lighten the load. Laughter is a beautiful thing! It looks like a rainbow and sounds like a mountain stream. It feels like a refreshing shower, softens our moods, sweetens our dispositions, sustains us when the going is rough. Learn to laugh together—joyfully!

Don't expect a perfect marriage. God makes it clear that none of us is perfect. Our righteousness is in Jesus Christ. For any couple to strive for a "perfect" marriage is a sad waste of valuable time—time that could be wisely spent in building a *good* marriage to the glory of God.

Be consistently grateful. You *can* change. The process may be long, even tedious, but the Great Designer knows what he's about. What we *have been* is never so important as what we may become. We cooperate in God's molding process not by nagging, but by nurturing. Not by needling, but by kneeling. Not by deflating, but by praising.

So thank God for every evidence of growth. Praise him, too, for all he will yet do.

Kristi, I can't wait to meet the special man who will be ready to learn these lessons with you!

Love, Ruth

The Story Inside

Dear Ruth,
I'd like to show you another poem. I guess it's because one of my "voices" says that "no one else could possibly understand...." I've had a close personal relationship with Jesus Christ since I was a little girl—I know you have too, so maybe you will relate to my problem. Somehow, I just can't imagine sharing my deepest, most intimate thoughts and fears with someone else besides God. I would feel so vulnerable, afraid of being rejected.

I know that Christian couples should be able to pray together and learn to merge their spiritual selves as well as the rest of their lives. I hope that when the time comes, I'll be able to do it. But the one thing that really scares me about marriage is—no secrets.

This is my poem:

> There's a story going on inside of me.
> While legs walk straight
> and arms hold books,
> a mouth smiles and talks.
> But there's more to me than that....
> A spirit inside, with a direct line,

a heart that's tuned to heaven
while feet stay pavement-bound.
Can you see, can you hear?
There's a story going on inside of me.

Do you think I'm ever going to be able to share that story?

Love, Kristi

Dear Kristi,
Oh, I do understand. And the kind of deep sharing of your inner life that you refer to takes time and commitment. If you were to ask me the greatest cementing force in our marriage, I would not say, "Well, we try to compliment each other every day. We share the work load; we talk things over." Nor would I say, "Rollie always opens the car door for me. We light a candle at the dinner table...."

All of these things have a definite place, and they *do* enhance a marriage. These little personal things show genuine caring. But the one consistent habit above all others that has drawn us closer to each other and to God is this: *From the beginning of our marriage we've kept prayer high on our priority list.* We've prayed *with* and *for* each other for thirty years.

Our day almost always starts with a cup of coffee and a few delicious morsels from the Bible. (Breakfast after that!) We've discovered that it's better to read five or six verses and *digest* them than to attempt three chapters haphazardly. We pray specifically. We ask God to enable us to apply what we've read as we face the demands of the new day.

Often we pray aloud as we walk together. I remember the sense of oneness we felt with our entire *neighborhood* the day we took turns praying for families whose homes we passed. We asked God to resolve conflicts and give guidance to parents and children. As we prayed for each marriage, we felt a sudden closeness toward mates who may never have prayed for each other.

Sometimes we pray while driving. As we share our personal longings and needs, Rollie's hand always reaches for mine. The sense of God's presence is so real. We *know* he's riding with us.

Once we stopped pulling weeds in our backyard. Under a warm August sun we asked God to clear the choking weeds from our hearts and make our lives more productive. (We were both feeling an emptiness at that time.)

We've sometimes roared with laughter when words haven't come out right—when crazy sentences sounded ridiculous. I think God laughed with us!

In Palm Springs there's a very special swimming pool. It doesn't look much different from a hundred other pools, but one September afternoon, surrounded by splashing vacationers, we talked to

God in that pool! We quietly thanked him for the glorious vacation he had given us—so relaxing, just what we needed.

Then there's our own "private" hill, which we found several years ago. The very first night we claimed it as our own—as our hilltop oasis. Every so often, when our attitudes need revamping, we find our way to our private hilltop. We look down over a vast expanse of shimmering lights. Here we pray for the people we love most. Here we recapture the incredible joy of renewed commitment to God.

Kristi, I know that most people have questions about prayer. We do, too. We're often mystified about guidance, about unanswered prayer, about God's will. All of us stumble over our doubts at crucial times.

But one thing we've learned in our marriage: When we determined to talk *with* God rather than *about* him—when we go to him as our loving Father simply because Jesus told us to—something happens in our lives and in our marriage.

"How do we start praying as a couple when we've never prayed with anyone?" This is a typical question asked by many. I understand it so well. Although family devotions were a daily pattern in our family, I suddenly realized after we were married that I'd never prayed with a *husband* before. Rollie had never prayed with a *wife* before.

This was a new kind of intimacy. Were we willing for this transparency in our marriage?

Yes, we decided, we were. Our love was deep and real, and we wanted God to be *first* in our home. So we began to pray, each in our own faltering way, with hesitant words and clumsy sentences. Short prayers. Jumbled thoughts. But we kept at it until praying together became a joyous adventure. Here is how we approach prayer, Kristi:

- In an unhurried way, we begin by expressing gratitude at mealtime. Bowed heads and clasped hands create a beautiful atmosphere of love and reverence. We take turns praying aloud. We seldom pray long prayers.
- Occasionally, we write our prayer requests. Then as we exchange lists, we pray silently or audibly for each other.
- Sometimes we pray without *asking* for anything. We just praise God as we wait silently in his presence. The Bible says praise delights God.
- We pray conversationally, each a sentence or two about one subject, talking to God personally and without pretense.
- We try to be specific and expectant.
- We listen to God! Prayer is two-way communication. God speaks in many ways, but most consistently through the Bible. Find your own method of study. We like to alternate—a

chaper in the New Testament and then one in the Old. Circle, underline, write on margins. Share your thoughts with each other.
- When you don't *feel* like praying, don't give up! Tell God about it. Often when we feel our need *least*, we need him *most*. God not only hears, he *helps*.

Kristi, when the time comes, you will be ready to *learn* to pray together. The story inside goes on and on—with two hearts instead of one!

Love, Ruth

Lord, Please Whisper a Secret

Dear Kristi,

Remember what I said in my last letter about *writing* my prayer requests? It's a wonderful thing to carry on a personal correspondence with the God of the universe! I've been doing this for years. I know you keep a prayer journal, too. I want to tell you how I got started.

I was probably eight or nine when my father called me into his office one day. In simple language he explained to a little girl God's method of communication—how he speaks to us through the Bible, through books and music and sermons, through people and circumstances; how he whispers secrets to anyone who will listen. I was fascinated! To think that the God who made the stars and sky and rushing seas would actually talk to *me!*

Dad told me that he often wrote down the thoughts that seemed to come from God as he prayed and read and studied. I was immensely challenged. *I wanted to hear secrets!* So that very week a little blue notebook became a book of secret prayers—childish, but honest. For example:

Dear Jesus,
Today you whispered a secret. I told a lie to my mother, and you said to say I'm sorry. Now I have a secret for you. I don't want to tell her yet, so please don't tell her before I do.

That was the beginning, Kristi. Since then I have filled many notebooks—red, blue, green, and yellow—with intimate thoughts expressed directly to God. There are several reasons why this practice has been profoundly valuable to me.

- My attention is focused on God. When I'm writing, there is not the muddled distraction of a tilted lamp shade, the crooked picture, the piece of lint on the carpeting.
- Distorted thoughts are crystallized and expressed coherently.
- A written prayer is a personal commitment not easily ignored or forgotten. God often reminds me of my written communication.
- As my sensitivity deepens, I am continually amazed at God's direct (and sometimes immediate) response to my heart's deep needs.

From time to time I have shared this method of prayer with close friends. A letter from my dear friend Janet says:

Dear Ruth,

I am recalling the days when I sat at your piano learning chords and arpeggios, but learning so much more, too. As much as I enjoy music, perhaps your greatest contribution to my life began the day you taught me to write my thoughts and longings to God, then to listen with pen in hand as the Holy Spirit reveals the will of the Father.

And now as a wife and mother, I daily meet challenges that are fully faced through this precious avenue of communion. When frustrations mount, he gives me wisdom I can refer to again and again.

Thanks for a gift that will bring lasting and growing fulfillment all the days of my life.

Love, Janet

Kristi, Janet was seventeen or eighteen when she began her prayer journals. I share her letter to encourage you to remember the joy that can come from keeping up your journal, no matter how busy you are.

I promised you I would share more from my journal, so I'm sending some thoughts from pages picked at random. This will give you something to read as a break from textbooks! (I hope you will see how my own inner story goes on, even within marriage.)

> Lord, everybody in the world ought to be singing the "Hallelujah Chorus" on a morning like this. All of nature exalts you—from the newest blade of grass to the tallest oak. And I? Well, I marvel at the Creator of it all!
>
> Today, dear Lord, I asked you how I could know if my surrender was complete. You said so simply, "How is it with you now—this moment? Settle it each moment, and you won't need to ask."
>
> Lord, yesterday at the sunny beach I traced little lines in the sand with a small twig. The wet spray blew against my face, and a thousand thoughts went tumbling into the waves. When I talked to you I heard you say, "My boundless love surrounds you."
>
> Today I am at home again—fixing meals, washing dishes, talking on the phone, answering mail—all the ordinary things, Lord. When I talk to you I hear you say again, "My boundless love surrounds you."
>
> And, dear God, suddenly I know it is as true today as it was yesterday!

How wonderful it is, Kristi, that we may talk to God about every detail of our lives, no matter how big or how small. It's not only that we *may*—he tells us that we *should!*

My prayers for you continue.

Love, Ruth

THREE

Real Love

Forgiveness Is a Beautiful Word

Dear Ruth,

Guess what? Steve is back in my life! I think I told you that we dated last year. I really don't know why we stopped—in fact, I waited and waited for the telephone to ring and finally realized it wasn't going to. I guess I was pretty hurt at first. My parents tried to help me understand that with his parents' separation, and all the needs of his mother and younger brother and sister, he probably just didn't have anything more to give at the time.

Anyway, just yesterday I got a letter from him, and he wants to come out to campus for a visit one weekend. (He's at a university about fifty miles away.) I was glad it was a note instead of a phone call, 'cause I had to think how I felt about him before I could answer! I do forgive him for his silence, but I don't think he really knows how I felt.

I started thinking a lot about forgiveness and about Steve, who has had to learn some heavy-duty lessons about forgiveness—especially toward his father. I guess people in a family have to forgive so that they can go on—but how much better if it happens *before* a break. I want to be understanding when I see Steve.

I wrote yesterday:

> Forgiveness is a path
> laid of stones that lead
> from me to you....
> I place each one down deliberately,
> edges touching, no mud oozing up between.
> Foot-sized, sturdy to walk on
> steps that get me there.
> God is building in my life,
> not just houses and gardens,
> but stepping-paths, too.

Love, Kristi

Dear Kristi,

Thank you for telling me about Steve. How wonderful that you're going to see him again!

Have I ever told you about Faye? And the lesson I had to learn about forgiveness?

Years ago when our family lived in Chicago, Faye and I were best friends. We walked to school together five mornings a week. We giggled and jumped rope and exchanged favorite books. We shared hair clips and diary secrets. Ours was a friendship of utter devotion.

When we were in the fifth grade, a lanky, blue-eyed boy stumbled (literally) over my desk one day.

He was pretty ho-hum, certainly no pacesetter, but he liked me and said so.

One day he handed me a note. "I like you, you're nice." Kristi, for me, the room turned upside down! I could hardly wait for the bell to ring. I *had* to ask Faye to be my maid-of-honor in ten years.

Then, out of the blue, the boy (I don't even remember his name) discovered Faye. She was prettier than I and far more adept at arithmetic. Result? In the middle of long-range wedding plans I lost the boy, and Faye lost her best friend.

Our friendship was shattered. We passed each other on the school grounds without a word. Our mutual friends begged us to make up, but we refused. Our alienation continued even after the boy was no longer important.

But finally at the end of the year, a week before summer vacation, Faye knocked at our back door. She said pleadingly, "Let's make up—please! You're still my very best friend."

Everything loving inside me wanted desperately to throw my arms around her. I ached to say, "You're my best friend, too!" But everything stubborn and selfish inside me refused to acknowledge love. I'd been hurt, and I assumed the frightening responsibility of punishing Faye.

When I saw her pushing back tears, I finally said, "Our family is going on vacation when school is out. *Maybe* I'll make up when we get home." Faye walked slowly toward her home—I can still picture her crossing the street.

We were gone three weeks—three miserable I-don't-like-me weeks. We hadn't been home more than five minutes before I rushed to the phone. My heart pounded. I *had* to talk to Faye. I wanted to shout at the top of my lungs, "You're my best friend, you really are!"

But Faye didn't answer the phone. A strange, unfamiliar voice said, "The Kimballs have left town—I don't have their address."

Kristi, my heart stood still. I'm not even sure if I said good-bye. I've suffered many times since that moment but never in quite the same way.

I've never seen Faye since the day she knocked at our door asking for my forgiveness. But often through the years I've thanked God for engraving upon my young heart a lesson I've never forgotten.

Someone said one day, "But you were so young, and it was just a little thing!" No, Kristi, unforgiveness is never a little thing. It warps and shrivels our souls. It boxes us in, and often it tears hearts and homes apart. It keeps us from wanting to pray. *We just have to forgive.*

You're probably thinking, "Did your childhood experience eliminate every future struggle? Is forgiveness always an easy thing for you now?"

Kristi, not for a moment am I suggesting that all grievances are as simple as a fifth-grade love triangle. Often forgiveness seems utterly impossible—*is* impossible, in fact, apart from God's grace. I pray that Steve's family, and especially his mother, will find that special grace.

Countless individuals have endured agonizing injustice. We do cruel and vicious things to each other. Often family members are demolished by unkind put-downs. Many husbands and wives become victims of infidelity or neglect or abuse. Even sarcasm and ridicule can be so damaging. Forgiveness is *not* always an easy thing.

Many times I hurt. I am a sensitive person—at times *touchy* might be a better word! I feel things deeply. Words and actions can cut. My inclination is to brood, to "suffer silently." But one truth is deeply ingrained within me: There is no hurt, no offense, no agony too great for God to heal! Whatever the cutting pain, the love of Jesus can withstand it! When we *ask* for the gift of forgiveness, God always says yes!

Kristi, forgiveness does not mean that we disregard an offense. To say, "Don't worry, it's all right," is often less than honest. Many things are far from all right.

Forgiveness simply means a deliberate release of an offense. We *choose* to forgive. We *accept*, we *release*, and we *drop the charges*—just as God, through Jesus Christ, dropped *all* charges against us.

Forgiveness frees us from a desire to "get even." Instead, it moves us away from our pain. We no longer wince or wallow in self-pity. We may *remember* at times (forgiveness may not always mean forgetting), but we are confident that God is weaving every memory into his glorious pattern for our lives!

To *ask for forgiveness* is the other side of the coin. Often it's easier to say, "I want to take you to dinner" or "I bought you a gift" or "Could I see you next weekend?" than to say, "I was wrong," "I was inconsiderate."

You see, Kristi, when we ask to be forgiven we do battle with our pride. But real healing cannot begin until we acknowledge our offense. To attempt to erase the hurt created by abuse or neglect is like splashing on perfume instead of taking a shower on a hot, humid day. The offense becomes more repulsive. We need cleansing! We need to be forgiven.

And sometimes we need to help each other apologize. Perhaps Steve needs your understanding in this instance.

My father often told a story of a husband who had deeply hurt his wife. Yet he found it agonizingly difficult to say, "I'm sorry." As a child he had been forced to apologize for offenses he had not committed. These experiences had damaged him emotionally.

The wife, understanding her husband's need, longed to help him. Finally, with her arms around him, she said gently, "Your eyes have that beautiful 'I'm sorry' look. I just want you to know that I completely forgive you!"

Forgiveness is a beautiful word!

Remember, Kristi, the important thing in an ongoing relationship is to make things right again, to restore the *relationship*. You have to look straight at the wrong, as Paul Tournier says, *see* it as wrong, and then forgive it. Sometimes you may even have to ask, "Will you give me the joy of forgiving you?" Why wait? Why build a wall around yourself? Why endure the fatigue and isolation that unforgiveness brings? Why freeze yourself in the unfair past? Why put off what must be done eventually if healing is to happen? God's gift of forgiveness is free—we only need to ask for it!

Years ago when I told Rollie about my friend Faye, he said, "Honey, let's never wait to forgive." We've kept our word! Once or twice we've stayed awake until 5:00 A.M. getting things settled, but it usually happened to be at a time when we could sleep a little later in the morning!

Our former pastor often said, "Keep short accounts with God." That has helped me so much. You see, there is simply no way I can keep short accounts with God and keep long accounts with the members of his family. None of us can. Jesus said so first: "Forgive, and you shall be forgiven."

Forgiveness is a beautiful word!

This is from my journal, Kristi:

> There is no hurt worth clinging to
> when I love you as I do!

P.S. Let me know how things go with Steve.

When the Door Says Welcome!

Dear Ruth,

It was so good to see Steve and really have a chance to talk. Some things seemed so much clearer now that we're both college freshmen away from home. Talking to an old *Christian* friend who also happens to be a very attractive man—well—I think I was able to know myself a little better as well as understand about Steve's struggles. He wants to see me again!

But I want to share something else with you that may not seem so important. All the time he was here, I wished I had something to offer of my *own*, a home with a couch, a stove, a table, and a pot of tea (like you gave me at your house, when we talked!). I guess I long for things to be settled—to have a *place* where I can grow and also be able to reach out to others. Do you think this has something to do with marriage, or vocation, or just wanting to be grown up too fast? Please tell me, is this normal?

Love, Kristi

Dear Kristi,

Yes, Kristi, your longing to be settled and to have a *place* to share is perfctly normal!

The week Rollie and I moved into our first *real* home, we had a party—even before we were half settled. We just couldn't wait! God had been good to us, and we wanted to celebrate. Everything was pretty chaotic. Dozens of things we needed were still missing. But nobody noticed—nobody cared.

Laughter and singing flooded every room. Ideas sprouted everywhere:

"Hey, you could hang your big mirror over the couch!"

"How about putting the rocker in the corner over there?"

"You sure could use some extra shelves in this closet."

Suggestions were frequent and free; we could take them or leave them. We were sharing God's goodness, and our hearts were brimming with joy.

After hot chocolate and crisp cookies, Rollie sang with gusto the old song "Bless This House." I secretly smiled. *Yes, Lord, please do!*

A little later we formed a circle of prayer—all of us—in the cluttered room, and everybody took turns praying. We dedicated our home to God— every room, every piece of furniture. Our home was his love-gift to us. Best of all, he lived with us!

My parents were with us that night. I'll never forget my father's prayer: "Lord, may everyone who enters this house learn a little more of your love—just by being here!"

Kristi, that's what hospitality is all about: God's love extended through us, where we live—in a single room or in a large two-story house.

Hospitality starts when the door says "Welcome," along with a wide-open heart and a friendly smile. Hospitality says, We care about you and we want you to know it!

Any home, however temporary, can be used for hospitality. Yes—even a dorm reception room—or perhaps a crowded kitchen, a candlelit restaurant table, a flickering fireside, a patio on a warm August night can be a place for friendship to bloom. The setting almost always takes more imagination than money. Small, intimate touches make for warmth and festivity, in August or December.

At our house friends often eat from salad bowls, bean pots, soup mugs, or even paper plates. We've had company for breakfast early in the morning. We've had midmorning brunches and tempting buffets and indoor picnics and waffle suppers and after-church chili feeds. Our patio comes alive with sizzling hamburgers and roasted wieners and sizable servings of spicy spaghetti.

Sometimes our friends sing their hearts out around the piano. Nobody ever wants to stop singing! Often we end the evening with crunchy apples and buttered popcorn—that's all.

Sometimes on guest nights we have soup and salad—and a fruit cup for dessert. Does it sound meager? Well, I make a *lot* of soup! We even play games now and then. One night somebody said, "I haven't had so much fun since I was a kid!"

Have you ever heard of graham crackers and spiced tea for refreshments? It happens once in awhile at our house! I like to frost the graham crackers. I light candles, too.

Gourmet dinners? Occasionally, but not often. Not anymore. You should have seen me entertain in the early years of our marriage. Fun? No, frantic!

I'd rush from morning until dinnertime. I'd plan elaborate five-course dinners with impressive menus. Exhaustion always numbed me afterward. We'd never have more than two couples at a time—we just couldn't! Not enough money or time or energy.

"Mother never told me entertaining would be like this," I'd complain. We'd always had company in our old-fashioned parsonages. It seemed so easy—for Mother!

One early morning while I was baking a peach cobbler for company, God caught me right in the middle of my muddle. He pointedly asked, "Do you want to *impress,* or do you want to *express* my love?" The question jolted me. I couldn't evade it. The sad truth was—I wanted to impress. Result: drudgery. Frayed nerves. A litany of lament.

Starting that day, God slowly revamped my

perspective. A mellow truth took hold of my heart: Jesus would have been content with crackers and cheese, had Martha joined Mary at his feet. I began to discover that the more *simply* I served, the more compassionately I cared.

Today the walls of our house can tell a thousand secrets. Between bites and sips we've laughed and cried. We've shared ridiculous jokes and shining memories. We've had challenging discussions; we've expressed creative ideas. We've prayed—so often we've prayed together.

One day my friend Donna said, "Ruth, it's funny, but I never seem to remember how your house looked after I leave. All I can think about is how warm and loved I feel when I'm there." All that day I thanked God for teaching me something about expressing his love.

Kristi, you need never apologize for a home or a room in which Jesus Christ delights to live. Simply expose your friends—old and new—to love, to caring. Help them to feel relaxed. I'm sure you *did* help Steve by your gentle spirit and caring attitude.

Maybe you can't entertain as you'd like to right now, but one thing you *can* do: You can open your heart as wide as you open your door. You can express God's love. You can radiate the compassion of Jesus Christ.

With every act of kindness you can say, "I care about you!"

You are learning many new lessons this year—

your first away from home. How happy I am to share some of my own experiences with you!

Love, Ruth

Listening Love

Dear Ruth,

I think I have a gift for listening. Does that sound funny? So many of the other women on my floor come in just to talk to me about problems—I sometimes feel I'm running a counseling agency. I share my faith with them, as much as is possible. I think they sense the peace that I have inside and would like to have it, too.

I felt it with Steve, too, that what he needed most of all was someone to listen. He did call last week again, and he's in the middle of exams. But he said we'd plan another time together soon.

This is from my journal:

God, you must like to listen, too, or you wouldn't ask us to pray. Help me to be open to hearing the hurts, the disappointments of others, and to reach out with your healing love. But heal me, too, Lord, so I can be a better listener! And help me to listen to my own heart as well, where you speak to me day by day. Amen.

Love, Kristi

Dear Kristi,

"Listening love" is a wonderful gift. Yes, you *do*

have it. After reading your letter I wrote in my journal:

> *Listening love is courteous. It says...*
> I will strive not to interrupt or correct or outguess you. I will not finish your sentences. I will not anticipate or break into your thoughts with "instant solutions."
>
> *Listening love is attentive. It says...*
> I will give you my full, undivided attention. I will not turn you off, walk out on you, or hide behind a smiling mask. I will not leave you isolated or busy myself with trivial things. I will strive to make our confrontation eye-to-eye, heart-to-heart, and love-to-love.
>
> *Listening love is kind. It says...*
> I will not overwhelm you with harsh, sarcastic retorts. I will not belittle or rebuke you. I will avoid unqualified terms like "you never..." and "you always...." I will strive to bring healing out of hurt, laughter out of tears, and understanding out of contention.
>
> *Listening love is objective. It says...*
> I will not attempt to *think* for you. I will strive to be informative rather than opinionated. I will not disagree with what you say until I am reasonably sure I understand what you mean.

Listening love is patient. It says...
I will not rush you. I will not insist on right-now conclusions. I will recognize the fact that two distinct opinions do not necessarily mean that one of us is wrong.

Listening love is sensitive. It says...
I will strive to listen to what you *do not* say—the feeling behind the words. I will attempt to "say back" what you have said, as I understand it. If, at a given moment, you cannot express your deep feelings, I will wait for you—as I would want you to wait for me.

Listening love is unselfish. It says...
I will guard against overconfidence, against pushy probing, against trite "spiritual answers," against wanting always to be right.

Listening love is confidential. It says...
I will never betray you. The secrets you have shared are locked in my heart. You alone know the combination.

Listening love is prayerful. It says...
Quietly, confidently, I will pray for insight, for wisdom, for tolerance. I will pray for the capacity to cope with the unpredictable. I will pray for gentle reactions. I will pray for sharing that does not count the cost or the return. I will pray above all for a love that intertwines with the love of God.

Listening love is growing. It says...
The more *dearly* I love you, the more *clearly* I hear you.

Kristi, it is important that friends express inner feelings and concerns to each other. We need to hear each other's voices and catch each other's smiles. And sometimes we need just plain ordinary chatter for a little while—without the burden of consuming problems! Wise old Solomon expressed it so aptly: "How wonderful it is to be able to say the right thing at the right time!" (Proverbs 15:23, TLB).

In puzzling moments with friends we may have to say, "Here we are, God, your little kids. Help us to grow up." And then we have to grow up, talkers and listeners alike.

Yesterday a letter came from my friend Kim. I want to share part of it with you. It expresses so beautifully what I've attempted to say.

> Sometimes I keep everything inside, trying to protect myself against hurt. But if you constantly cover your true feelings, it's like putting a drop cloth over a beautiful chair. Sure, it won't get soiled, but you see only the form of the chair. You miss all the texture and beauty.
>
> I want to experience all my heavenly Father has for me, and I can't do that with a drop

cloth over my heart. So he'll just have to see that the paint drips land in the right spots to blend with his pattern. I'm sure he will!

         Good-night, Kim

Kristi, listening love helps us to forget the drop cloths and let the lessons go on!
 I pray for you daily as you live out your calling on your campus with your friends and acquaintances this year.

           Love, Ruth

Take the Time

Dear Ruth,

I need help! Is there some way to organize your life so that you have time for all the things you really need to do? I always seem to be just a little bit behind on everything.

How do you do it, as a busy wife and speaker and writer too? If I can't learn *now* how to be efficient, what chance do I have of *doing it all* later after I'm married and have someone else to think of too?

I was going to write a poem about time—but I didn't have time! *Sigh*. I love you.

Kristi

Dear Kristi,

Some people are marvelously able to bounce out of bed in the morning all nice and smiling while the sun is still yawning. My mother was like that. Every morning at six o'clock she'd be in the kitchen shuffling pots and pans, cheerful as could be.

I began to see early in our marriage (about the third day) that it would be a long time before I'd be up to Mother's level of discipline. I missed that word in a spelling contest once, and I was still struggling with it. Most of my problems evolved around the management of time.

You should have seen me clean house! It wasn't that I minded the tedious work. I flew from kitchen to bedroom, from scrub cloth to dustcloth, from drawers to cupboards, from clean sheets to silver polish. First the broom, then the vacuum, here a little, there a little, never completing any job before starting something else. If all of this suggests some frightening neurotic tendencies, I obviously had them. But be encouraged, Kristi, I've improved!

After one day of utter confusion Rollie said, forcing a smile, "Honey, have you ever thought of making a list?" I was sure he meant a grocery list. My mind began racing—what in the world had I forgotten *this* time? But he was definitely talking about a time schedule. Slowly it dawned on me that I was sadly disorganized.

Several weeks later, while I was grating carrots for a salad, I suddenly happened to remember a theme I had written in high school entitled, "If I Had Time." My teacher's comment, written neatly across the top of my paper, left its indelible mark: "Why don't you *take* time?"

For the next hour or so I gave some serious thought to my poor planning and flimsy excuses. I realized that I could never box up time to save for a rainy day, nor could I retrieve it, or pull a weighty chunk of it back when it slipped by me.

Starting that night I began to write in my journal

what God seemed to be saying to me regarding the sacred use of his gift of time. I'm sharing a few of the thoughts with you today, not because they are spectacular or new, but because I believe the principles are valid:

Take time to practice the presence of God. You are unique. God has made you different from anyone else for his own purpose. Don't copy; don't compete; don't be bound by the opinions of others. No one can determine God's schedule for you.

Take time to plan your day wisely, under God's direction. (What thoughts come steadily, repeatedly, convincingly?) You can do everything you *ought* to do. Seek God's "oughts," then follow his guidance. Offer every responsibility, tiny or tremendous, as a love-gift to him.

Take time to make realistic work lists. Discipline yourself. Avoid procrastination. The key word is *now.* Action creates feeling. Work by a time schedule. Finish one task before starting another. Don't ask for more time. But ask for wisdom to do what you *ought* to do in the time you have.

Take time to learn the warning signals: Are schoolwork and activities crowding your time for inner development? Are you tense, indifferent, irritable? Are you playing the martyr? Are you unforgiving? Are you careless about your appearance? If so, you are too busy.

Take time to learn the decisive, deliberate answer: no!

Take time to anticipate interruptions. They will come. Accept them as part of God's training program.

Take time to "Commit your work to the Lord, then it will succeed" (Proverbs 16:3, TLB). What you honestly commit, he takes. Whatever he touches, he changes.

Your choices during these college years will make some drastic differences in your life. But God can give you fresh insights. His own word of promise is: "And your ears shall hear a word behind you, saying, 'This is the way, walk in it,' when you turn to the right or when you turn to the left" (Isaiah 30:21, RSV).

Kristi, when you hear that word, clearly and consistently, take the time.

Love, Ruth

FOUR

Waiting Is Hard

It Will Be Worth It . . .

Dear Ruth,

You have shared with me so many wonderful things about your marriage, and the joy and fulfillment of knowing God's way—with both partners seeking to do his will. But as you know, so many couples today don't wait for marriage to live together. Many of the women who tell me their stories have had sex with boys since they were young teens. Now, the mood on campus is more cautious because of fear. Unfortunately it has taken something like AIDS to make people rethink free sex.

I haven't even really dated a lot—my parents have been very protective. And they knew I intended to wait, to get an education, and to *prepare* for marriage, important as it is, especially to Christians who want to make a commitment for life!

I'm so thankful that there is something worth waiting for because waiting *is* hard. Sometimes I envy those who seem to find love so easily and give themselves so casually. It is wonderful to be loved and needed, and I want that closeness to another person—a special man. Frankly, I'd love to have it now!

I keep telling myself it's worth the wait, but I need to hear it all again from someone who understands how I feel and can help me sort this out. I sometimes dream about Steve and wonder if we will fall in love. But his parents' problems, I think, are keeping him from trusting his own feelings too much, and I doubt that he thinks about marriage in the romantic way I do. Has the world changed that much?

Please tell me if I'm right.

Love, Kristi

Dear Kristi,
Yes, it *will* be worth waiting for. I'm so happy for the chance to talk to you about this intimate side of love and marriage.

Your sexuality is a great gift. In God's glorious creative plan such a union encompasses your total being: soul, spirit, body. Sex is intended to be a vital expression of the self within. It pervades every particle of personality. In the mysterious oneness of the sex act, the most intimate form of communication possible, you and your husband will someday be saying to each other in a thousand secret ways . . .

> I want you to know me, all of me, as I really am. I long to know you, all of you, as you really are. I am now and always a part of you. You are now and always a part of me. I give

myself to you willingly, unreservedly, in full confidence of our love for each other.

Sex, *as God intended it*, Kristi, is rich and refreshing. It is stimulating and rewarding. It is longing and belonging.

Sex, *as God intended it*, is total giving and accepting. It is trustful mutuality. It is a tremendous drive, a powerful source of unity. It is the cooperative experience of meeting each other's stirring needs.

Sex, *as God intended it*, can be timid yet daring, awkward yet bewitching, comforting yet susceptible to tears.

At times, Kristi, it races breathlessly up a windswept hill. At other times it is as quiet as dawn.

It can banish loneliness and recapture wholeness. It can shatter restlessness and create incredible closeness.

Sex, *as God intended it*, is a language all its own, expressed in an environment of warmth and understanding. It is so much more than moments of passion—it is a promise of fidelity. It is more than a passing episode—it is a sharing of life. It is creative rather than destructive. It delights rather than defrauds.

Sex, *as God intended it*, is a glorious celebration—a celebration of "the wonder of us" ... the wonder of God! It is a dynamic gift to be treasured and cherished. It is a lifelong partnership with One whose plan is wonderfully wise and good.

The Bible makes it clear that God planned the magnetic attraction between the sexes. The reasons are explicit: The joyful expression of complete oneness. Mutual delight and release. Procreation.

It is always true that apart from God's standards, sex can become grossly selfish and frustrating. Even ugly and frightening. Today, when there is so much muddled thinking about sex in our society, God's imperatives have not only been pushed aside, but rudely ignored. The results are sad. What was once a priceless gift is now, in too many instances, a cheap commodity. Death and disease are a tragic part of the picture, bringing threats of overwhelming stress and fear.

We need to know that God is never out to cheat or frustrate us, nor does he fling his commands to thwart the very needs he himself created. With our sadly misguided concepts today we seem to have forgotten that his goal is our highest good in *every* specific—including sex. For every "thou shalt not" he graciously offers a counter "thou shalt have."

Kristi, if you can genuinely praise God for the gift of your sexuality, you will draw strength to wait for the right expression of it within your marriage someday.

Anything that originates with God just has to be good!

But there are also lessons to learn.

I wonder, do you happen to have any of your old assignment books from piano lesson days? Probably not. You were a little girl when I was your teacher, and many years have escaped since then. But you may remember that I always included a list of Helpful Hints with each new assignment: Count out loud! Watch your fingering! Observe the rests! Increase the tempo! Every week I'd write a new list, and the exclamation points were always intentional.

Once when I was writing out your assignment, you surprised me by saying, "I really like the Helpful Hints. They help me remember." (I honestly think you were the only student who did!)

Here is another list—a list that has nothing whatever to do with piano lessons.

I'm eager to share some guidelines, some basic reminders, relating directly to sexuality in marriage.

Some time ago Rollie and I wrote this pledge— in fact we have read it together as a *prayer!*

Loving Each Other As We Do
A Sacred Pledge

Loving each other as we do . . .
We acknowledge our sexuality as God's priceless gift—this unique plan for our fulfillment and unity.

It is our personal desire to bring honor to God and wholeness to each other in the physical expression of our love.

We will accept our emotional and biological differences, believing that God has made us uniquely male and female.

We recognize that in each of us there are secret chambers: memories, voices, impressions, childhood echoes....

Loving each other as we do...
We will permit God to use our conflicts and differences to teach us his peace. With loving patience, we will support each other in our gradual growth as a couple.

We will each focus on the other as a person, not as a pleasure—as a trust, not as a gimmick.

We will seek to delight rather than to demand, to give rather than to get.

Loving each other as we do...
We will regard our physical intimacy as the true expression of a love already existing between us—never as a path leading to love.

We will share the defeats as well as the victories, the awkward moments as well as the blissful.

We will not insist on perfection—rather we will strive for growth. We will not compete for the mountaintop—rather we will climb the mountain together.

We will lift our hearts in a celebration of gratitude for God's marvelous love, which makes our love possible.

Loving each other as we do...

Yes, Kristi, it *is* worth waiting for!

Learn to Be Happy with More

Dear Ruth,
Yesterday I wrote this poem:

> My future is like a castle
> glistening from afar.
> It beckons me, with promises
> like coins not yet in my pocket.
> The present is more of a hut
> or bungalow by a stream—
> temporary shelter, adequate heat, light—
> no more than I need, and no less.
> Is it wrong to want more?
> To want to get "there" sooner?
> I guess that depends on what road I take.

Ruth, your words about marriage and sex add to the "glisten" of that castle—but I know that for me it is still very far away. I'm sure it isn't wrong to have dreams and hopes. Right now, I wish I had my own place, my own money. Of course, I'm working on my degree so that I *can* earn enough to support myself in a few years. I want to learn the lessons that I need now, while I'm still dependent on my parents' support and having to *wait* for so many things I'd like!

Did you ever feel that way? Does it get better?

Love, Kristi

Dear Kristi,

Yes, I *do* know how you feel.

And I did have to learn to wait—even *after* I was married.

In fact, I had to learn the hard way.

Our apartment was located within walking distance of church, school, and town. We didn't have a car then, but it didn't matter. It took me about ten minutes to walk to the center of town where I could gaze wistfully and longingly at all the dress shops with their fashionable window displays. I decided I needed the exercise—frequently.

One day, in the window of one of the most elite shops, there appeared a dream-dress that absolutely had my name on it. Everything about it was perfect: color, size, design—*everything*. I could tell it was right even before trying it on. Some things you just *know*.

Kristi, I had never in my life opened a charge account. I was reasonably convinced, however, that it was a simple, painless procedure. You probably signed your name on a few blank lines, you gave several impressive references, and you walked out with the dress. After all, I reasoned, *I was married now,* and every wife should experience the elementary exercise of opening a charge account. It was a matter of responsibility! Besides, I was tired of waiting until we could *afford* things.

The store manager happened to be a member of our church. She immediately recognized me, so there was no problem whatever. She was kind, solicitous, and very complimentary. It all turned out beautifully—exactly as I had anticipated. The dress fit perfectly! Signing my name came easily—it was fun to write *Mrs.*—and the box was light enough to carry away with a song.

But that night after I modeled the dress (Rollie liked it!), we had a long, detailed discussion about budgeting. The thrust of our discussion was: I wasn't working then. Rollie was working, but he was going to school, too. As it happened, the dress was three times more expensive than our clothes budget allowed—with or without a charge account. I sat there sorting my mixed emotions during our lengthy conversation. Kristi, it was such a *beautiful* dress.

Rollie didn't insist that I return the dress. He simply asked, with a little bit of a smile, "Do you really think you'd enjoy wearing it?" So what would you have done, Kristi? Probably exactly what I did. The next day I walked back to the shop (slowly) with the box under my arm.

Well, we've come a long way since then. But I still often have to *wait* for what I'd like to have *today*. (And I still think I've never seen a prettier

115

dress than the one I reluctantly returned that long-ago day!)

Almost all people—even wealthy people—want more than they have!

Kristi, I personally believe that the one and only way to deal with our desire to have things now is to make God our partner in our finances as well as in every other aspect of our lives. When he is our center of reference, we can learn to live in the here and now. Sure, problems still exist. We're faced with a constant barrage of them—including financial problems. But we have the spiritual insight to cope, at least we begin to develop it. That's the big difference.

Does it disturb you when I say that (married or single) you will *never* have any money of your own? Rollie and I won't either. You see, life is a trust from God, and *all* that we have is his. Think about it a minute: What do any of us have that God didn't first give? Really, nothing.

What are some of the money traps we fall into so blindly?

Keeping up with the Joneses. Many people simply can't handle prosperity—especially the prosperity of the person next door. To try to keep up with the Joneses is both foolish and futile. Just suppose we finally make it. Around the corner live the Smiths. So it starts again—the competition.

Poor management of funds. Installment buying and personal loans can get out of hand quickly if we let our emotions rule us. Wise budgeting is a must for economic security. It allows for daily expenditures. It allows for systematic giving and saving, for transportation, for insurance, for unforeseen emergencies. Budgeting also includes long-range planning. It includes paying off loans as quickly as possible and keeping accurate records for income taxes.

Money management is no easy thing. It involves discipline and control. It means commitment. It requires the ability to face responsibilities. I agree with the experts who say that money management is basically self-management. We tell much about ourselves by the way we handle money.

The "my money" syndrome. It's important to learn financial integrity now, while you are single. You will need such honesty in marriage. There are husbands and wives who have no idea how much money their mates earn. Vaguely, perhaps, but not totally. One wife confided that her husband had gotten three raises without her knowledge. She said, "I only know now because my husband's partner mentioned it inadvertently one day."

Another wife said, "I never tell my husband what I pay for things. If an item costs ten dollars, I tell him I paid five for it. He doesn't tell me how he spends money—so why should I tell him?"

Countless money quarrels result simply because mates think *me* instead of *we*. Mutual trust is shattered. One friend of mine said caustically,

"We'll never be married financially."

Years ago Rollie and I "agreed to agree" on the distribution of funds. I don't check with Rollie every time I buy clothes or gifts or household items. When one of us comes home with something new, we don't say, "Now before we eat dinner I'd better explain that I paid exactly $6.99 for this." It just isn't that big a deal. We both know our budget—and we try to stay within it. The only time I say excitedly, "How much do you think I paid for *this*?" is when I have found some terrific bargain.

Charge accounts? Yes! But we set limitations. When large items are involved—like furniture and appliances and cars—we look, we consider, we decide together. We don't purposely hide expenditures—that's the principle. The key word is *honesty*.

At our house Rollie keeps the financial records—by mutual agreement. He is decidedly more adept in this area than I am. In hundreds of homes, perhaps most homes, the wife is the head bookkeeper—more power to her. How fantastic to be so capable! *Who* takes the responsibility is not as important as *how* it is done.

The "someday" syndrome. Someday, when we've bought a bigger home, when we've put in our swimming pool, when we've settled on a new boat, when we've taken our big trip, *someday* we'll *give* more—we really will. We'll even give 10 percent of our income. But right now there are so many pressing things, and well—it would be such a struggle. We really can't afford to tithe.

But when giving becomes primary, and getting becomes secondary, we begin to see things from God's point of view. The promise of Jesus is direct: "For if you give, you will get! Your gift will return to you in full and overflowing measure, pressed down, shaken together to make room for more, and running over" (Luke 6:38, TLB). So learn to give until it no longer hurts.

Now for a few general practicalities:

Determine a budget. When you begin to work, start a tithing and savings program. A good basic goal is 10 percent to God and 10 percent to savings. Start with your first paycheck. Distinguish between your wants and your needs.

It's a great idea to make friends with your piggy bank. For years we've had an almost sacred agreeement about dimes. We don't spend them. Every summer our dimes make a sizable dent in our vacation expenses.

Learn to be happy with—*more.* More music and laughter, more conversations, more friendships, more positive attitudes, more faith in God's lavish provision. All of these gifts are free!

One thought about gratitude: You can never be thankful enough—but you can keep on trying!

Love, Ruth

It Takes a Lot of Little Things

Dear Ruth:

Steve and I have been seeing more of each other lately—it's even better than I had hoped, at this point. He seems more relaxed, glad for the friendship, as I am. But I just don't know what comes next. I'm afraid I might spoil what we do have by doing something stupid! We have so little time to be together and do things. I want to make everything count.

Can you help me?

Love, Kristi

Dear Kristi,

I want to dedicate this letter to "the praise of little things"! They are the small touches that keep a relationship healthy and growing.

At first, Kristi, it seems so easy in a love relationship—almost effortless much of the time. The little courtesies, the happy glances, the unexpected surprises ... they come so naturally. But to keep it from bogging down, to keep from gradually taking each other for granted—that's the real challenge. I want to share some lessons Rollie and I have learned together.

Little surprises have flavored our joy.

I've discovered that I still have a lot of little girl in me when it comes to surprises. The very word *surprise* worked its own magic during my childhood. I vividly remember my mother's mysterious way of making trivial things unbelievably exciting. She'd whisper, "I have a surprise for you!" and I would be filled with anticipation. Mother even made creamed spinach sound exciting by calling it a surprise.

Early in our marriage, Rollie and I centered in on the Surprise Game. I don't know exactly how it started, but I *do* know we're both sweepstakes winners at it.

I love Rollie's reaction when he finds a mystery package on his desk, especially after a long, tedious day. The gifts are never elaborate—a pair of socks, maybe, or a bottle of after-shave lotion. He's even excited when he finds a couple of candy bars tied with a huge red bow. Sort of ridiculous? Maybe. But fun, too.

There was that day Rollie came home with an apple corer for me—*his* idea of a surprise. Somehow, he just couldn't fathom me going through life without an apple corer. Now using an apple corer requires apples—and there I was with my shiny new gadget and not an apple in the house. Life happens that way sometimes. One thing calls for another.

Well, nothing else would do. Rollie dashed to the

store and came back with the biggest, juiciest apples he could find. We had ourselves a coring party to surpass all parties. Then for four or five days we ate baked apples. Funny thing about that corer—I still have it, and it's one of my favorite gifts.

I could go on telling you about the ridiculous, sweet, unusual, sentimental surprises we've brought home over the years—but you can work on your own ideas.

Traditional days are memory banks.

If you ever want an unusual recipe for charcoal turkey, just talk to me. Our first Thanksgiving dinner was downright catastrophic. But right in the middle of company dinner, somebody at the table (I don't remember who) hit on the idea of thanking God for the "charcoal turkeys" in our lives: the difficult things, the seeming disasters, that God actually used for our good. As we shared together that day, an aura of gratitude surrounded the table. It was indeed a therapeutic hour. Every year since, we've taken time on Thanksgiving Day to thank God for the "charcoal turkeys" of the past year.

I've lost track of the times we've made our own valentines. Rollie is the artist (not me), so his valentines are much more professional. Usually I just write a note with hearts scattered all over the page. Does it take time? Well, yes—thoughtful things do take time. Love takes time!

A Journal of Joy records our gratitude.

After hearing a challenging sermon on gratitude one Sunday, we were shamefully aware of our lack. Too often we take God's goodness for granted. As we drove home, an idea crystallized: We decided to keep an accurate two-month record of the day-by-day *unanticipated* joys God sent our way. I was elected recording secretary. Here's a sample of an "ordinary" week.:

- Beautiful, unexpected letter from my sister Rainy. Her loving words sing in our hearts. Thank you, Lord.
- Sheila left some fresh flowers at our door with a darling "Sheila-note." Thank you, Lord.
- The dentist's bill was less than we expected. Amazing, Lord. Thank you.
- You blessed us so much as we read your Word today. Thank you, Lord.
- Pinki brought me a delicate butterfly necklace—a reminder of the cover of my first published book. Thank you, too, Lord.

Kristi, the experiment was transforming! We learned some valuable lessons: God is infinitely aware of little things; he so often blesses us through others; and gratitude dispels doubt. It increases our faith. A thankful heart is a peaceful heart.

Renewed goals flavor all of life.

Years ago we adopted a three-step plan for the first day of each new year:

From our reading, we choose three Bible promises. We personally claim them for the new year, asking God to fulfill them in *his* way. We put no time limit on them, nor do we dictate the terms. We simply accept his Word. *We are promise-oriented.*

We write down three personal goals for our individual lives. We share them, pledging prayerful support to each other in our endeavor to achieve. *We are goal-oriented.*

We commit the year totally to God, always expecting much from him. *We are God-oriented.*

We have followed this plan through the years. The result? God continues to surprise us with joy. Not happiness always, but joy. Happiness depends upon circumstances. Joy rests only on our relationship with him.

Kristi, there are so many more things I could share with you, but I'm writing today to stimulate your thinking as you pray about the future God has for you, one that will be beautifully unique.

Let's give thanks together for "little" things!

Love, Ruth

In This Place, In This Hour

Dear Ruth,

As the semester pushes on, and especially as I've been dating Steve more steadily, your letters have come like a fresh breeze of love for me!

There *is* much to look forward to. But also a lot to enjoy right now! As I was reading over your letters, I notice how practical it all is—learning to live with God and with other people—in this moment.

Please keep sending me your thoughts—I need help every day!

Love, Kristi

Dear Kristi:

I think you have hit on exactly the right point. We *all* need help every day. Christianity *is* for this very moment if it is for any time at all.... I tried to capture that truth in several poems of mine. I'd like to share them with you today.

Today, Lord
Yesterday, Lord
when you asked what I wanted
above all else

I said I wanted to be
exclusively yours.
Today, as you startle me
with opportunities—
keep me from begging off
until tomorrow.

Fruitless Hours
My Lord
forgive me for spending
so many fruitless hours
debating, analyzing, mulling over
what I think I should do
in future years—
when again and again
you have proven
that the hours of each *today*
lived in explicit obedience
reveal sufficient spiritual insight
to make *tomorrow* surprisingly clear.

Sure Guarantee
Early this morning, Lord
as we read your Word aloud
you captured our attention
with the psalmist's declaration
"Oh, magnify the Lord with me
and let us exalt his name together."
My husband said thoughtfully
"If we'll do it day by day—
if we'll really exalt his name *together*

we'll have a sure guarantee
for a *forever* marriage."
The thought became a melody
singing in my heart all day.
Lord, that's why I felt compelled
to write today's date
and the words *forever together*
in the margin next to the verse.
Now help us to do it.

Kristi, it is always rewarding to live in God's *now.* We're so inclined to think "someday," forgetting that as we learn to trust God day by day, moment by moment, he is silently planning in love for us. I hope that reminder will encourage you this very day.

Love, Ruth

Once in a While

Dear Ruth,
It is almost semester break—and am I ready! I'm so tired of having to be at an eight o'clock class three times a week, staying up late nights studying for exams. A break is exactly what I need.

Steve is going to drive home with me—he and a friend are coming to pick me up next Friday. And soon I'll get to visit with you, dear Ruth. Can we have tea together again? There are many more things to talk about now, aren't there?

Do you ever feel like throwing it all over and just being lazy? I confess I do. I hope that's not wrong. Wow, am I ready for a break!

See you soon!

Love, Kristi

Dear Kristi,
I want to tell you about a time when *I* needed a break.

On a clear, bird-singing Sunday of my twelfth year, I didn't want to go to church. That was all there was to it. I hadn't "backslidden," I wasn't coddling a pent-up rebellion, nor was I exhibiting a dangerous streak of independence. I just didn't want to go to church.

The warm sun streaming through the windows added a quiet charm to our old house. I pictured a simple, leisurely day away from school and church and "have-to" things. I could sing my heart out at home if I wanted to—and if I didn't want to, I was sure God would keep right on loving me.

But how to broach the subject, how to explain my childish longing and be understood—that was the turmoil spinning inside me. After all, preachers' kids always went to church—just as regularly as they went to school. More regularly, in fact. In school you at least had vacations!

As I stood in the warm kitchen watching my mother peel potatoes to add to the roast, thoughts kept tumbling. My secret longing persisted. Finally I just blurted it all out—how I wanted to stay home, how I didn't think God would mind a single bit.

Mother kept right on peeling potatoes. Not once did she interrupt me. Not a word about how I was disappointing her. She listened attentively, quietly, and somehow I sensed that she understood. When the last potato was peeled, she wiped her hands on her blue apron. Then very gently she put her arms around me.

"Honey," she said calmly, "you know we can't always do what we feel like doing. Nobody can. We would hurt ourselves and lots of other people, too."

Well, that settled it, I thought. I knew what was

coming. Of course I'd have to go to church. It was silly even to talk about it.

Then suddenly I heard, "But once in a while we can! Once in a while we need a change. Once in a while we can do what we want to do—just because we want to. It's all right—you may stay home this morning."

I'll never forget that special Sunday and my peaceful sense of aloneness. Mother came home after Sunday school. When she asked how it felt to stay home alone, I couldn't explain my exhilaration—but I think she knew. We talked and laughed—and God was right there.

Kristi, the memory of that day is still fresh and vivid. In fact, my whole life has been enhanced by it. Not because I stayed home from church, but because I learned a profound principle: *Once in a while we can!*

Once in a while we can get away from alarm clocks, phones, peanut butter jars, milk cartons, schoolbooks, schedules . . . away from the competitive workaday world—a world that threatens and grabs and pushes and clobbers.

Once in a while we can find a quiet spot—a cabin or a camper or a desert motel—away from nerve-shattering pressures and family and friends. Every now and then we need to reevaluate and rediscover the simple joys. We need to step out of our ruts and moods. We need to capture the magic of life again!

Once in a while even a husband and wife need to be away from each other! Too often we lose the capacity for personal enjoyment. We need time to play alone, to pursue individual interests. We need to express our own God-given creativity. In marriage, togetherness becomes stronger when we're proud of our mate's personal achievements, when we can share our own talents.

Once in a while we need to walk alone, think alone, pray alone. We need solitude and silence. God wants to hear our own private secrets. He alone can fully satisfy the deep longings of our hearts. We are unique in his sight. Our strengths, our skills, our abilities are wonderfully *ours*.

Once in a while we need the luxury of a day or an evening we can call our own. Fishing . . . hiking . . . shopping . . . painting . . . driving . . . *enjoying* . . . without qualms, without guilt.

Once in a while it's good to get away! To forget? No, to fortify. To spend money foolishly? No, to invest wisely all that we have.

Once in a while we can.

Kristi, I pray for you in all your *nows*, in all your *once in a whiles*, and in all that God has in store for you.

I'll be glad to see you during your semester break. Yes, we certainly *can* have tea together. If you'd like, we'll talk some more about love and the things that make it work.

In God's good time, Kristi, you will be standing

at the altar promising to love, comfort, and honor the man by your side. You will know without a doubt that this is the man you want to commit yourself to once and for all. Your heart will sing as you begin a life journey *together*.

Until then, keep growing! Keep trusting!
You are loved!

Ruth

Other Living Books® Best-sellers

THE ANGEL OF HIS PRESENCE by Grace Livingston Hill. This book captures the romance of John Wentworth Stanley and a beautiful young woman whose influence causes John to re-evaluate his well-laid plans for the future. 07-0047 $3.95.

ANSWERS by Josh McDowell and Don Stewart. In a question-and-answer format, the authors tackle sixty-five of the most-asked questions about the Bible, God, Jesus Christ, miracles, other religions, and creation. 07-0021 $4.95.

THE BEST CHRISTMAS PAGEANT EVER by Barbara Robinson. A delightfully wild and funny story about what happens to a Christmas program when the "Horrible Herdman" brothers and sisters are miscast in the roles of the biblical Christmas story characters. 07-0137 $3.95.

BUILDING YOUR SELF IMAGE by Josh McDowell. Here are practical answers to help you overcome your fears, anxieties, and lack of self-confidence. Learn how God's higher image of who you are can take root in your heart and mind. 07-1395 $4.50.

THE CHILD WITHIN by Mari Hanes. The author shares insights she gained from God's Word during her own pregnancy. She identifies areas of stress, offers concrete data about the birth process, and points to God's sure promises that he will "gently lead those that are with young." 07-0219 $3.95.

COME BEFORE WINTER AND SHARE MY HOPE by Charles R. Swindoll. A collection of brief vignettes offering hope and the assurance that adversity and despair are temporary setbacks we can overcome! 07-0477 $6.95.

DARE TO DISCIPLINE by James Dobson. A straightforward, plainly written discussion about building and maintaining parent/child relationships based upon love, respect, authority, and ultimate loyalty to God. 07-0522 $4.95.

DAVID AND BATHSHEBA by Roberta Kells Dorr. This novel combines solid biblical and historical research with suspenseful storytelling about men and women locked in the eternal struggle for power, governed by appetites they wrestle to control. 07-0618 $4.95.

Other Living Books® Best-sellers

DR. DOBSON ANSWERS YOUR QUESTIONS by James Dobson. In this convenient reference book, renowned author Dr. James Dobson addresses heartfelt concerns on many topics including marital relationships, infant care, child discipline, home management, and others. 07-0580 $4.95.

FOR MEN ONLY edited by J. Allan Petersen. This book deals with topics of concern to every man: the business world, marriage, fathering, spiritual goals, and problems of living as a Christian in a secular world. 07-0892 $4.95.

FOR WOMEN ONLY by Evelyn and J. Allan Petersen. Balanced, entertaining, diversified treatment of all aspects of womanhood. 07-0897 $5.95.

400 WAYS TO SAY I LOVE YOU by Alice Chapin. Perhaps the flame of love has almost died in your marriage. Maybe you have a good marriage that just needs a little "spark." Here is a book especially for the woman who wants to rekindle the flame of romance in her marriage. With creative, practical ideas on how to show the man in her life that she cares. 07-0919 $3.95.

GIVERS, TAKERS, AND OTHER KINDS OF LOVERS by Josh McDowell and Paul Lewis. This book bypasses vague generalities about love and sex and gets right to the basic questions: Whatever happened to sexual freedom? What's true love like? Do men respond differently than women? If you're looking for straight answers about God's plan for love and sexuality, this book was written for you. 07-1031 $3.95.

HINDS' FEET ON HIGH PLACES by Hannah Hurnard. A classic allegory of a journey toward faith that has sold more than a million copies! 07-1429 $4.95.

HOW TO BE HAPPY THOUGH MARRIED by Tim LaHaye. One of America's most successful marriage counselors gives practical, proven advice for marital happiness. 07-1499 $3.95.

JOHN, SON OF THUNDER by Ellen Gunderson Traylor. In this saga of adventure, travel with John—the disciple whom Jesus loved—down desert paths, through the courts of the Holy City, to the foot of the cross, leaving his luxury as a privileged son of Israel for the bitter hardship of his exile on Patmos. 07-1903 $5.95.

Other Living Books Best-sellers

LIFE IS TREMENDOUS! by Charlie "Tremendous" Jones. Believing that enthusiasm makes the difference, Jones shows how anyone can be happy, involved, relevant, productive, healthy, and secure in the midst of a high-pressure, commercialized society. 07-2184 $3.50.

LORD, COULD YOU HURRY A LITTLE? by Ruth Harms Calkin. These prayer-poems from the heart of a godly woman trace the inner workings of the heart, following the rhythms of the day and seasons of the year with expectation and love. 07-3816 $3.50.

LORD, I KEEP RUNNING BACK TO YOU by Ruth Harms Calkin. In prayer-poems tinged with wonder, joy, humanness, and questioning, the author speaks for all of us who are groping and learning together what it means to be God's child. 07-3819 $3.95.

MORE THAN A CARPENTER by Josh McDowell. A hard-hitting book for people who are skeptical about Jesus' deity, his resurrection, and his claim on their lives. 07-4552 $3.95.

MOUNTAINS OF SPICES by Hannah Hurnard. Here is an allegory comparing the nine spices mentioned in the Song of Solomon to the nine fruits of the Spirit. A story of the glory of surrender by the author of **Hinds' Feet on High Places**. 07-4611 $4.50.

NOW IS YOUR TIME TO WIN by Dave Dean. In this true-life story, Dean shares how he locked into seven principles that enabled him to bounce back from failure to success. Read about successful men and women—from sports and entertainment celebrities to the ordinary people next door—and discover how you too can bounce back from failure to success! 07-4727 $3.95.

THE SECRET OF LOVING by Josh McDowell. McDowell explores the values and qualities that will help both the single and married reader to be the right person for someone else. He offers a fresh perspective for evaluating and improving the reader's love life. 07-5845 $4.95.

THE STORY FROM THE BOOK. The full sweep of **The Book**'s contents in abridged, chronological form, giving the reader the "big picture" of the Bible. 07-6677 $4.95.

Other Living Books® Best-sellers

STRIKE THE ORIGINAL MATCH by Charles Swindoll. Many couples ask: What do you do when the warm, passionate fire that once lit your marriage begins to wane? Here, Chuck Swindoll provides biblical steps for rekindling the fires of romance and building marital intimacy. 07-6445-5 $4.95.

SUCCESS: THE GLENN BLAND METHOD by Glenn Bland. The author shows how to set goals and make plans that really work. His ingredients for success include spiritual, financial, educational, and recreational balances. 07-6689 $4.95.

THROUGH GATES OF SPLENDOR by Elisabeth Elliott. This unforgettable story of five men who braved the Auca Indians has become one of the most famous missionary books of all times. 07-7151 $4.95.

WHAT WIVES WISH THEIR HUSBANDS KNEW ABOUT WOMEN by James Dobson. The best-selling author of **Dare to Discipline** and **The Strong-Willed Child** brings us this vital book that speaks to the unique emotional needs and aspirations of today's woman. An immensely practical, interesting guide. 07-7896 $3.95.

WHY YOU ACT THE WAY YOU DO by Tim LaHaye. Discover how your temperament affects your work, emotions, spiritual life, and relationships and learn how to make improvements. 07-8212 $4.95.

You can find all of these Living Books at your local Christian bookstore. If they are unavailable, send check or money order for retail price plus $1.00 postage and handling per book (U.S. and territories only) to:

Tyndale D.M.S., Box 80, Wheaton, IL 60189

Prices and availability subject to change without notice.

Please allow 4-6 weeks for delivery.